Carrot Predicament

by Mar'ce Merrell
illustrated by Barbara Hartmann

[redacted]

A Hodgepog Book

Hodgepog Books and The Books Collective acknowledge the ongoing support of the Canada Council for the Arts for our publishing program. We also acknowledge the support of the City of Edmonton and the Edmonton Arts Council.

Editor for the press: Glen Huser.
Managing Editor: Mary Woodbury
Cover illustration and inside illustrations by Barbara Hartmann.
Cover design by Chao Yu. Inside design and page set-up by Ike at the Wooden Door, in Times New Roman and Palatino.

A Hodgepog Book for kids.

Published in Canada by Hodgepog Books, an imprint of The Books Collective, 214-21, 10405 Jasper Avenue, Edmonton, Alberta, Canada T5J 3S2. Telephone (403) 448 0590, fax (403) 448 0640.

Canadian Cataloguing in Publication Data

Merrell, Mar'ce, 1966-
Ben and the carrot predicament

ISBN 1-895836-54-9

I. Hartmann, Barbara, 1950- II. Title.
PS8576.E738B46 1998 jC813'.54 C98-910747-7
PZ7.M541Be 1998

DEDICATION

I dedicate this book with love to my sources of inspiration: Callie, Cameron, Chris, Andrew and Benjamin, and to Dennis for his never-ending love and support.

One

WHISKERS AND EARS

"Ben, it's time to get up. You have thirty minutes to get ready for school. There's fresh carrot muffins," Ben's mother called.

Carrot muffins—again! Ben rolled over on his back. That makes carrots every morning this week. No wonder I dreamed about carrots all night, Ben thought. He pulled back his *Space Galactica* bedspread. He sat up, rubbing his eyes.

He found one slipper on the floor. He couldn't see

the other one. He got down on his hands and knees to search. He moved a pile of *Junior Scientist* magazines and his spaceship models. He found the bag of carrot cookies he had been hiding under the bed. He didn't find his slipper.

"Ben! Your juice is ready! Twenty minutes." His mother was at the bottom of the stairs. She'll be up here any minute if I don't get moving, Ben thought.

Ben took the slipper off and trudged to the bathroom.

He searched for his toothbrush, his nose twitching, his whiskers wiggling.

Wait a minute! WHISKERS?!

Ben inspected his image in the mirror. Above his top lip, right under his nostrils, were six hairs, three growing out of each side. Ben rubbed his finger over them. They were about the length of his big toe, Ben figured, only thinner. Like the fishing line Dad kept in his tackle box. Rubbing them tickled. He gave them a good scratch. He looked in the mirror again. They were still there.

Ben's head itched too. He scratched one side of his head and then the other. What he felt made him scream.

"Oh no, I'M A RABBIT!"

"Ben?" His mother knocked on the door. "Ben? Are you all right? Is something the matter?"

Oh no.

Ben froze. He stared at himself in the mirror.

What am I going to tell Mom? he thought.

How do you tell your mom you've turned into a rabbit?

Two

HIDING THE EVIDENCE

"Ben? Ben? Open this door." Ben heard his mother twisting the door knob. He sprang into action.

"No!" Ben rushed to the door and pushed in the lock. "Everything's fine, Mom."

"Okay. Well, hurry up, Ben. You need to drink the carrot wheat-grass juice right after it's squeezed. It's more nutritious that way," his mother said.

Ben sat down on the edge of the tub.

"What am I going to do?" He took three deep

breaths. He felt as if someone had just crunched his favourite space model. He couldn't tell what the pieces were or how to put them back together.

"First I need to find out what's happened." Ben remembered that in Junior Scientists Club the first step was gathering data.

He stood up to the mirror.

He felt the brown fur-covered ears that had popped through his curly brown hair. They were warm and hurt a little when he pinched them. Fuzzy, too. Like the skin of a peach.

"Whiskers and ears—they appear to be of the rabbit variety," he said. He lifted his top lip.

"Front teeth appear to be normal."

He jumped as high as he could. It wasn't any higher than the day before. He sniffed the air. He smelled the same thing he did every morning, his father's awful after shave and his mother's flowery soap.

"No unusual rabbit-like abilities," he decided.

He reached behind him, afraid of what he might find attached to his backside.

"Whew!" he sighed. "At least I don't have a tail!"

"Now what?" Ben said, his rabbit ears bobbing in the mirror. "Of course. Hide the evidence!"

Ben took his dad's electric razor out of the cupboard. He turned the water on full blast to cover up the buzzing noise. He stretched his top lip down as far as he could, and closed one eye. Ouch! It hurt a little.

"Cool." He was finished. He could just barely feel where the hairs had been.

Ben grabbed a towel off the rack and piled it on his head as he'd seen his mother do.

"Getting rid of these things might be a bit tricky. I'll have to wait until after school to work on that."

Ben held on tight to his terry cloth turban as he dashed across the hallway to his bedroom.

Three

BAD HAIR DAY

Ben wore his favourite baseball cap down to the breakfast table, the ears tucked underneath. His father sat at one end of the table, his head behind the newspaper.

Ben stared at the glass of brown juice sitting in front of him. Ever since Mom started this weird diet two months ago, she was making him eat vegetables in everything. She added carrots to cookies, muffins and pancakes. Ben didn't mind that. He loved carrots. But brown-coloured carrot and wheat grass juice was going too far.

Ben lifted his glass. He took a deep breath. He gulped the juice down in one slurp.

"Oh! GROSS!" he spluttered.

"Benjamin!" His mother stared at him.

"Son, mind your manners," his dad said through the newspaper.

"Sorry. The taste surprised me," Ben said.

"Ben?" His mom stood next to him. "Is something wrong with your hair? Why do you have that cap on?"

"No, Mom. I'm just having a bad hair day. Besides, wearing a cap is cool." Ben chewed quickly on his carrot muffin.

"Is there something you're not telling me Benjamin? You didn't dye it blue like Robbie, did you?" Mom had her hands on her waist. Ben gulped. He stared down at his plate, shaking his head. "No. I didn't dye it."

"Benjamin? What is going on with your hair?" He

couldn't tell her. She'd freak over blue hair. Rabbit ears would make her explode.

"Mom. It's nothing; really. It's just...It's just..."

She started tapping her right foot on the floor.

"It's just..." Ben looked up at the ceiling.

"I don't want Jennifer to see my hair like this," he lied. His stomach felt weird.

He didn't want to lie to his mother and he certainly didn't want her to think he cared what Jennifer thought.

"Oh Ben. That's so sweet." His mother leaned over and kissed his cheek.

"It's nothing, really." Ben felt his ears tingling.

Four

THINKING TROUBLES

Going to school with rabbit ears wasn't as bad as Ben thought. Nobody noticed. Nobody said, "Hey why are you wearing that cap?" or "What you got under there?" or "What's with your top lip? It looks strange."

When Ben went to the bathroom all he could see was a lumpy hat and whisker stubble.

When he was in class all he could think of were his

ears and whiskers. It was all that thinking that got him into trouble.

"Benjamin Peters? Benjamin?" Ben heard Mrs. Fox's voice. It sounded far away but, when Ben looked up, she was standing in front of him.

"Benjamin have you heard a word I've said?"

"Yes, ma'am." Ben's voice shook a little.

"Well, then, who is the main character of the story I just read to the class?"

Ben stared at the paper in front of him. He'd drawn pictures of a boy with rabbit ears and whiskers. He flipped it over.

"The rabbit?" he answered. He heard the boys behind him snickering.

"Good one, Ben," someone whispered.

"Nice try, but there was no rabbit. The main character was Jonathan."

Ben stared at the ceiling trying to remember the story.

"Now Jonathan had a problem," Mrs. Fox continued. "I will give you one more chance, Benjamin. Can you tell me what Jonathan's problem was?"

"Uh...Uh..." Ben struggled.

Problem...Problem...Problem—the word echoed in his head.

"The problem was those darned ears and whiskers," Ben blurted. The whole classroom erupted in laughter. Ben's ears tingled.

"Very funny, Benjamin." Mrs. Fox marched back to her desk. "We'll talk some more about this after school."

Ben's stomach felt like it was full of butterflies and jumping frogs.

SA

Five

COSTUMES

"Okay Benjamin."

He was sitting on a chair next to Mrs. Fox's desk.

"What is going on? What's all this rabbit talk?"

Ben couldn't answer. He stared at the floor, wishing he could disappear.

"Are kids teasing you?"

Ben shook his head.

"Is everything okay at home?"

Ben nodded.

"Are you sick? Do you have a fever?" Mrs. Fox lifted her hand to feel his forehead. Ben panicked. She's trying to take my hat off, he thought.

"I feel fine." Ben pushed her hand away just in time. "I'm just...I'm just..." Ben looked around the room. He saw the black cat decorations Mrs. Fox had put up for Halloween.

"I'm just excited about Halloween," Ben lied. He could feel his stomach begin to grumble. "I'm sorry about today."

"Halloween? I see. Well, I don't want to see this behavior again."

Ben nodded his head.

"I'd like you to work on the party invitations with Peter before you leave." Mrs. Fox patted Ben's shoulder.

Ben pulled his hat down tight, took three deep breaths, and joined Peter at the computer.

"Mrs. Fox says we have to remind everyone—no peanut butter," Peter said.

"Why no peanut butter?" Ben asked.

"Because Jordan's allergic." He pulled Ben closer to him. "He might turn into an elephant if he eats any peanuts!"

Ben laughed. Peter was always cracking jokes.

"So what are you going to be for Halloween?" Ben asked. "A clown?"

"No. My mom can only make capes," Peter said. "I'm going to be a super hero.

"I'm going to have laser vision, super strength and smelly arm pits." Peter held his arms like a wrestler, flexing his muscles.

Ben plugged his nose. He laughed until his face hurt.

"What are you going to be?" Peter asked.

Ben was going to tell him. He rubbed the space under his nose and straightened his hat. He didn't say anything, though. He was afraid Peter would tease him.

"Oh, I don't know." Ben rubbed his top lip.

"Probably some kind of animal." His ears started tingling.

"My mom makes great rabbit ears." Ben's stomach rumbled so loudly he was afraid Peter would hear it.

Six

JUNIOR SCIENTIST

When Ben got home he found a note:

Dear Ben,
I'm at the beauty salon getting my hair done. I'll be home at 5.
Have some cookies.

Love,

Mom
p.s. Your latest Junior Scientist *magazine arrived. It's on your bed.*

"Cool!" Ben ran up the stairs to his bedroom.

Ben looked forward to getting his *Junior Scientist* magazine every month. It always had stories about famous scientists, new scientific discoveries and even a science experiment you could do at home.

"Amaze your friends! Make things disappear!" Ben read on the cover of the magazine.

He turned to the experiments page. It read:

If you've got a problem hiding your secrets, try this experiment to create hidden messages.

Ben read that sentence over. He read it five more times.

"If you've got a problem hiding your secrets..." Ben whispered. He scrambled through his desk, searching for paper and a pencil.

He copied down the list of materials he needed.

He raced to the bathroom and the kitchen, getting everything on the list. He made a quick trip to Mom's studio for a paintbrush. He knew he shouldn't.

"Benjamin. These are not brushes to play with," she said the last time he had used them. "These brushes are for serious work."

"Painting my pet rock was playing. Getting rid of

rabbit ears is definitely serious work," Ben reasoned.

When he got back to the bedroom, he glanced at his clock: 4:20 p.m..

"Forty minutes to get back to normal," he said. "That's not much time."

Ben pulled his *Junior Scientist's Experimental Lab* out from under his bed. His mom got it for him for Christmas. The last time he used it, he dyed the carpet in his bedroom green. She told him he couldn't use it again without adult supervision.

"This is an emergency, though," Ben muttered.

Ben read the instructions in the magazine quickly.

He poured ingredients into one glass to make solution A. Then the rest of the ingredients into a second glass labeled solution B.

Ben took his hat off and got to work.

He took Mom's paintbrush and painted one ear from bottom to top, front to back. Then he brushed the other ear, top to bottom, back to front. He waited. Nothing happened. He ran into the bathroom.

The ears were still there!

Seven

THE EXPERIMENT

"Oh no!" Ben groaned.

He watched the ears sway back and forth when he shook his head. He jumped up and down, flinging his head this way and that. When he looked in the mirror, the ears were sticking up.

"It's no use." Ben's eyes filled with tears. "I can't get rid of these things."

"Wait a minute!" He remembered. "What about solution B?"

Ben slammed his bedroom door behind him. He was going to read over the instructions just one more time. He looked at the clock. 4:50 p.m.

"Not enough time!" Ben stirred the paintbrush around in solution B.

He wiped down one ear top to bottom, front to back. He brushed the other ear, bottom to top, back to front. He waited.

His ears did not tingle.

His head did not feel lighter.

He reached up. They were still there.

"Oh. It didn't work!" Ben stared at the scientific solutions on his desk. "What do I know about science? All I did was dye the brush...blue?"

Ben picked up his mom's favourite paint brush. It was blue.

"Blue? How did this turn blue?" Ben turned it over and over in his hand. "Mom's going to kill me. I dyed her favourite brush blue."

Ben sat on his bed, scratching his head, trying to figure out what he had done. He rubbed his ears.

"Wait a minute! If the brush is blue, then..." Ben jumped up. He ran into the bathroom.

"Oh No! I don't believe it. BLUE EARS."

"Ben, I'm home..." It was Mom.

He grabbed a towel and piled it on his head.

"I'm just getting out of the shower," he yelled from the top of the stairs. "I'll be down in a half-hour."

"Okay. Ben? How was your day? Anything exciting happen?"

"No. Nothing exciting," Ben called back. Dying your rabbit ears blue isn't exciting, he thought. It's terrible, horrible and awful.

Eight

NO MORE CARROTS

Ben joined his parents at the dinner table. His hat was fixed firmly onto his head, backwards. Ben picked at the carrot-broccoli casserole on his plate.

"Ben is there something wrong?" his mother asked. "You usually love this casserole."

"I need some help, Mom," Ben said. "I need you to help me with my Halloween costume. The party's on Friday."

"Ben that's two days away," she said. "Why didn't you tell me before?"

"Well, I thought I was just going to be a Dracula like last year but I changed my mind. I want to be a rabbit." Ben felt his cheeks turning red.

"A rabbit. Aren't you a little old to be dressing up as a rabbit?" She put her napkin on the table. "Are you sure you're all right?"

"I say let Ben decide what he wants to dress up as. There's nothing wrong with rabbits." Dad winked at Ben.

Ben took another bite, waiting for his mother to speak.

"I can make a rabbit suit. I guess it makes sense that you want to dress up as a rabbit. You eat so many carrots I wouldn't be surprised if you turned into a rabbit."

Ben's fork stopped in mid-air, halfway to his mouth. Ben stared at his mother. She was stabbing another bite of carrot with her fork.

"Mom what did you just say?"

"I said it's okay that you want to dress up as a rabbit."

"No, not that, the other part."

"Oh, you mean the little joke?" She wiped her mouth with her napkin.

"Yeah, that's the part. What was it again?" Ben asked.

"You never laugh at my jokes." Mom smiled at Ben. "You really thought it was funny?"

"What was it?" Ben demanded.

"I just said that you eat so many carrots, you'd probably turn into a rabbit." She smoothed the napkin on her lap.

"I don't want any more carrots." Ben pushed his plate into the center of the table.

"Not for dinner, not in muffins and definitely not in my juice."

"But Ben, you love carrots. They're so nutritious. I read a study the other day that said if you eat carrots every day then..."

"Mom," Ben interrupted. "I think I'm allergic. I don't want any more carrots. I've eaten lots already."

"He's right," Dad added. "I agree with him. I've had enough carrots, too. Surely we can eat something else that's healthy."

"What would you like then?" Mom stared first at Dad, then at Ben. "If you don't want carrots?"

"Bananas," said Ben. "I like bananas."

Nine

THE ALIEN RABBIT

Ben washed his ears twenty times between the night he turned his ears blue and the day of the Halloween party. The ears were still the darkest, deepest blue, like the sky just before the stars come out. Ben pulled the rabbit costume his mother had made him over his clothes. It was very furry and he immediately started to sweat. Ben waited until he heard the bus. He ran down the stairs.

"Ben, you haven't eaten any breakfast. I'll drive you

to school today," his mother yelled as Ben streaked by her in the kitchen.

"It's okay, Mom. I'll just eat one of these muffins you made for the party. I gotta go." Ben thought he was going to make it out the door without her seeing him. He was wrong.

"Ben! What on earth do you have on your head?" His mother stood with the dishtowel looped over her arm, her hand on her hip.

"What?" Ben asked.

"Those blue things on your head. Where did you get them? Why are you wearing them?"

"They're ears." Ben shrugged his shoulders. "I'm a rabbit. Remember?"

"A rabbit with blue ears?" His mother's eyebrows ran into each other as she frowned.

"I'm... I'm..." Ben heard the bus honking. "An alien rabbit." He grabbed his books and ran as fast as he could to the bus.

SCHOOL BUS

Ten

THE HALLOWEEN PARTY

Ben was the only rabbit at the Halloween party—alien or not. All the kids liked his costume. Ben liked not having to wear his hat. It felt good to let his ears bob and sway.

Peter came as Rope Man. He was completely purple; shirt, pants and cape. He even had his face painted purple.

He had gold ropes winding around his waist and legs. He wore a purple cape with gold ropes flying from the neck.

"Does Rope Man have smelly armpits?" Ben asked.

"You wanna smell for yourself?" Peter lifted his arm. Ben backed away.

"Boy, your mom did a good job on your costume," he said and reached up to touch Ben's ears.

"Hey, they feel like real rabbit ears. They look like them too, except for the blue dye. They're even warm. How did she do that?" Peter said.

"Oh. Uh. My costume is so hot even my ears are sweating." Ben's cheeks turned red.

"Cool. Let's eat." Peter ran like a speeding bullet to the food table.

"Hey Ben. Where's your favourite carrot chocolate chip cookies? You are a rabbit, aren't you?" he called.

"I'm not into carrots anymore. Mom sent banana muffins instead." Ben answered.

"Now we'll have the prizes for costumes." Mrs. Fox announced.

Jennifer got the prize for the sweetest costume. She tiptoed to the front of the room. Her purple skirt with the silver stars glued all over it fluffed up and down as she moved.

"Attack of the smelly armpits." Peter called out as she passed him.

"Peter. Please come up here." Mrs. Fox was not smiling.

"It is my pleasure to give Peter this award." Mrs. Fox put her arm around Peter. He was grinning from ear to ear.

"Peter's super powers include knocking out bad guys with one sniff of his arm pit. His award is for the most revolting costume this year," Mrs. Fox said.

Ben burst into laughter.

"Yes!" Peter held up his arm in victory. Ben pinched his nose.

“The most original costume goes to somebody who’s been acting very original lately.” Mrs. Fox held out a huge bucket of caramel popcorn. “Benjamin wins first prize for his Alien Rabbit costume.”

Ben’s ears rang from the applause.

Mrs. Fox bent down to whisper in his ear. “How did you get those things stuck on? Those ears look absolutely real.”

“You wouldn’t believe me if I told you,” Ben answered.

Eleven

CARROT DREAMS

Ben sat at the dinner table working up courage. Courage to tell his parents the truth about his ears. He was on his third helping of curried rice with bananas. His parents were talking about buying a new stereo.

"Mom. Dad." Ben cleared his throat. "About these ears..."

"Yes dear, they're lovely. Very original." His mother

smiled at him. “I see you like them so much you haven’t taken them off.”

“Son, I think you hit on a great costume idea. Down

at the office we have a costume party once in a while. Do you think I could borrow your idea?"

Ben gulped. "Yeah, sure."

"You think we should get a CD player that holds ten discs? How much more is that going to cost?" his dad asked his mom.

Ben took his plate up to the counter.

"I'm such a coward," he thought. He walked up to his bedroom. "I'll have to wait until tomorrow when they aren't so busy."

Ben got into his pajamas. "It's not going to matter if I wait one more day."

He smoothed out his ears and turned out his light.

Ben dreamed he was sitting in a garden. Carrots were all around him. They covered his legs and feet. Ben picked up a bundle of carrots and threw them over the fence. He picked up another bunch and threw them into a huge hole in the garden. Flying carrots filled his dream.

Twelve

THE TRUTH

"Ben, I've got some banana pancakes for you." Ben's mother was outside his bedroom door.

"No thanks. I'm not hungry." Ben rolled over and covered his head with the blanket. He didn't want to see his parents.

"Come have breakfast with us, Ben," Mom said. "It's Saturday."

"Okay," Ben mumbled. He knew he couldn't wait any longer. He had to tell them the truth today.

Ben searched the floor for his slippers. He found the first one under his *Junior Scientist* magazine.

"The other one must have disappeared," Ben sighed. "Too bad I wasn't as lucky with the ears."

Ben trudged into the bathroom. He opened the cupboard, searching for his dad's electric razor. He turned on the water. He pulled his top lip down and... What?

No whiskers! Where did they go?

Ben rubbed and rubbed and couldn't feel anything.

"They're gone!" He yelled.

He looked in the mirror.

The ears were gone, too!

Ben scratched his head all over. He turned his head from side to side, looking for ears.

They had disappeared.

Ben ran down to the breakfast table. He wanted to celebrate. Then he saw his mother's face. She had her lips pressed together. Her eyebrows were pushed into each other in a deep frown.

"Benjamin Peters," she said. "Do you know what

happened to my favourite paint brush?"

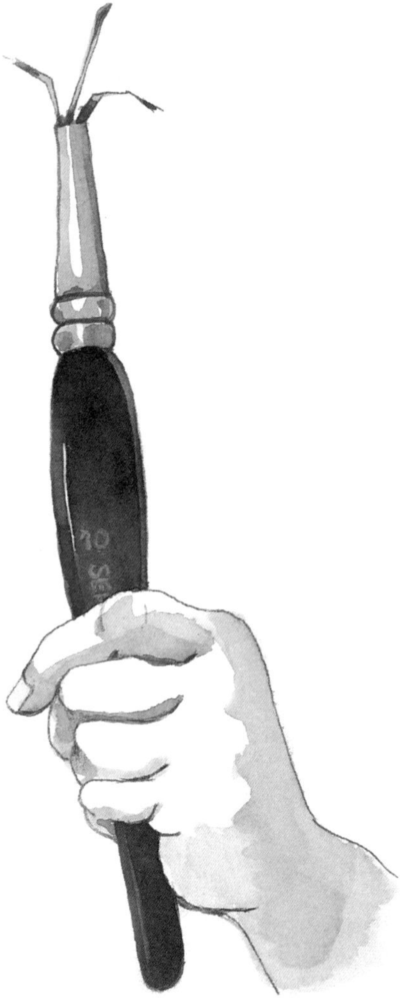

She held up the paintbrush Ben had used in his science experiment. All of the hairs were missing.

Ben choked on the orange juice he was drinking. Juice spluttered out of his mouth and onto the tablecloth.

"I...I..." Ben looked up at the ceiling. His stomach ached. "I'm sorry, Mom. I used it for a science experiment."

"Well what do you plan to do about this?" His mother shook the brush in the air.

"I'll buy you a new one," Ben suggested.

"Have you got a hundred dollars?" she asked.

"No. I've got $50 in the bank and I'll do whatever you want to make up the other $50," he said.

His mother clucked her tongue.

"That sounds reasonable," she said finally. "But no more. No more science experiments and no more using my brushes."

"Don't worry, Mom." Ben smiled. "I don't want to do any more experiments like that one."

Ben's mother went back to adding carrots to the juicer. She insisted on eating them even though Ben and his dad had stopped.

"Son, your mother and I have noticed you've been acting a bit strange. Is there a problem?" Dad poked his head out from his newspaper.

"No. No problem." Ben shook his head.

"You know you can tell us the truth." His dad smiled. Ben grinned.

"We're always here to listen." Dad went back to reading.

Ben considered the truth. How can I tell them the truth when I don't know for sure what the truth is? I could say I grew rabbit ears, I turned them blue and I made them disappear. But did I make them disappear? Was it the science experiment? Was it cutting out carrots? Was it that dream?

"Mom?" Ben took his plate into the kitchen.

She finished rinsing off the carrots and put them on the counter.

"The truth is..." Ben stopped. He saw something on his mom's upper lip.

"Come here." He motioned for her to come closer. He could see six hairs, three growing out of each side. They looked like the fishing line dad kept in his tackle box.

"What is it?" she asked.

"Mom, I've got to tell you something." Ben could see two brown tips on the sides of her head. "You're not going to like it."

"HUH? What's all this about?"

"I think you better stop eating carrots, Mom," he said.

"Why, Ben? I don't understand."

"I didn't either." Ben shook his head. "But I think you might be allergic to carrots, like me."

"What makes you say that?" she asked.

Ben knew he had to tell her the truth. He took a deep breath. He couldn't feel any jumping frogs or butterflies in his stomach.

"When *I* discovered my whiskers and ears..." he began.

About the Author

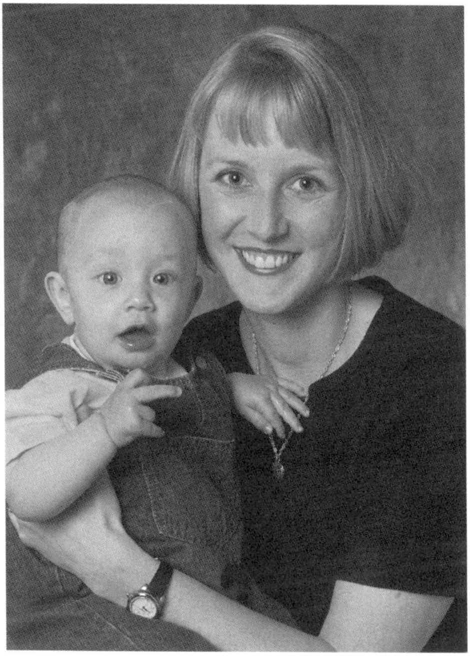

Mar'ce Merrell is a mother, wife and writer. She is eager to read her first novel, *Ben and the Carrot Predicament,* to her youngest son Benjamin. Ben's brothers Andrew, Cameron and Christopher, his sister Callie and dad Dennis help in caring for Ben so that Mar'ce can work on her next writing project, a novel for middle readers. The family lives in a very cozy home in Edmonton.

About the Artist

Barbara Hartmann has illustrated many children's books, including *Purple Hair, I Don't Care* (Stoddard, 1994), *the Abaleda Voluntary Firehouse Band* (Treefrog, 1990) and *Fishes in the Ocean* (Fitzhenry & Whiteside, 1998). She has also illustrated other Hodepog Books, including *A Gift for Johnny Know-It-All,* 1996, and *Getting Rid of Mr. Ribitus,* 1998. She lives in Edmonton with her husband Peter Kazsor and son Daniel.

If you liked this book...

you might enjoy these other Hodgepog books:

Read them yourself in grades 4-5, or read them to younger kids!

A Gift for Johnny Know-It-All
by Mary Woodbury, illustrated by Barbara Hartmann
ISBN 1-895836-27-1 Price: $5.95

A Real Farm Girl
by Susan Ioannou, illustrated by James Rozak
ISBN 1-895836-52-2 Price: $6.95

Arly and Spike
by Luanne Armstrong, illustrated by Chao Yu
ISBN 1-895836-37-9 Price: $4.95

Mill Creek Kids
by Colleen Heffernan, illustrated by Sonja Zacharias
ISBN 1-895836-40-9 Price: $5.95

A Friend for Mr. Granville
by Gillian Richardson, illustrated by Claudette MacLean
ISBN 1-895836-38-7 Price: $5.95

Ben and the Carrot Predicament
by Mar'ce Merrell, illustrated by Barbara Hartmann
ISBN 1-895836-54-9 Price: $5.95

Getting Rid of Mr. Ribitus
by Alison Lohans, illustrated by Barbara Hartmann
ISBN 1-895836-53-0 Price: $5.95

---

and for readers in grades 1-2, or to read to pre-schoolers:

Summer With Sebastian
by Gwen Molnar, illustrated by Kendra McCleskey
ISBN 1-895836-39-5 Price: $4.95

Teachers Guides Available. Write or fax:
Hodgepog Books, 214-21 10405 Jasper Avenue, Edmonton, Alberta, Canada T5J 3S2, ph. (403) 448 0590 fax (403) 448 0640